ON SAFARI

by Claire Watts
Illustrated by Louise Voce

KU-376-190

2	Introduction
4	Lions
6	Elephants
8	Giraffes
10	Rhinos
12	Hippos
14	Zebras
16	Ostriches
18	Gorillas
20	Chimpanzees
22	Safari Quiz
24	Index

TWO-CAN

In Africa there are lots of wild animals. Many of them live on the open plains. People take trips called safaris to watch the animals.

LIONS

Lions live together in groups known as prides. Two or three male lions, some lionesses and some cubs make up a pride.

Lions spend most of the day sleeping. Some lions sleep in trees.

Male lions have a hairy mane around their head and neck.

Lions eat a big meal every few days. The male lions always eat first, and the cubs eat last.

Lions from the same pride greet each other by rubbing cheeks.

ELEPHANTS

Elephants are the largest animals that live on land.

Elephants love water. They suck up water in their trunks and shower themselves.

Elephants use their tusks to strip bark from trees to eat. They also use them to defend themselves.

Elephants use their trunks like hands. They can pick up huge logs or tiny leaves quite easily.

Baby elephants suck their trunks, like babies suck their thumbs.

GIRAFFES

Giraffes are the tallest animals in the world.

Giraffes have small horns on their heads. These are covered in skin and look like small antlers.

When giraffes drink, they have to stretch their front legs wide so that they can reach the water.

Giraffes sleep during the hottest part of the day. Most giraffes sleep standing up, but some lie down.

Giraffes use their long necks to reach leaves high up in trees.

RHINOS

New-born rhinos do not have horns. Their horns start to grow when they are a few weeks old.

Rhinos use their strong horns to dig up trees so they can eat the roots.

Rhinos have very tough skin. They use their horns to defend themselves against attackers, but they usually run away instead of fighting.

Rhinos wallow in mud to keep themselves cool in the hot sun.

HIPPOS

Hippos have very heavy bodies. They move much more easily in water than on land.

Small birds keep a hippo clean. They pick insects off its skin, and out of its ears and nostrils.

Hippos often lie down in the water, with only their eyes, ears and nostrils showing above the water.

Hippos have huge teeth. They use their teeth to defend themselves.

Hippos can walk along on the bottom of a lake or river.

ZEBRAS

Zebras live in herds. They roam across the open plains eating grass and leaves.

Zebras use the tuft of hair at the end of their tail to get rid of flies.

Zebras have short, thick manes which stand up on their necks.

Zebras have wide black and white stripes. When zebras are gathered in a group, it is difficult to tell one from another.

OSTRICHES

Ostriches are the biggest birds in the world. They cannot fly but they run very fast.

Ostriches dig a nest in the sand to lay their eggs. Three or four ostrich mothers lay their eggs together.

Baby ostriches have spotted down on their necks.

Ostriches have long eyelashes to protect their eyes from dust.

GORILLAS

Gorillas live in forests, where they can find plenty of fruit, leaves and twigs to eat.

Young gorillas like to play follow-the-leader in the trees.

Female gorillas and young gorillas like to climb trees, but fully grown male gorillas are much too heavy to climb.

When gorillas are angry, they beat their chests with their fists. This makes a sound like a drum.

CHIMPANZEES

Chimpanzees live together in large family groups. They talk to one another by using their hands, and by making faces.

Chimpanzees are good at climbing trees. They build nests in trees to sleep in at night.

Chimpanzees usually walk on all fours. They stand up when they want to look around.

Chimpanzee babies ride under their mothers' bodies or on their backs.

Chimpanzees sometimes eat ants. They use long sticks to reach into ants' nests.

SAFARI QUIZ

What is a family of lions called?

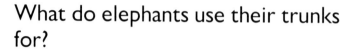
What do elephants use their trunks for?

How do chimpanzees talk to each other?

When does a gorilla beat its chest?

Where do ostriches lay their eggs?

How do giraffes drink?

What do you think a hippo's favourite place is?

What do zebras eat?

INDEX

chimpanzee 20
elephant 6
giraffe 8
gorilla 18
hippo 12
lion 4
ostrich 16
rhino 10
zebra 14

First published in Great Britain in 1991 by
Two-Can Publishing Ltd
27 Cowper Street
London EC2A 4AP
in association with Scholastic Publications Ltd

Copyright © Two-Can Publishing Ltd, 1991
Illustrations copyright © Louise Voce, 1991

Printed and bound in Hong Kong

2 4 6 8 10 9 7 5 3

All rights reserved. No part of this publication may be reproduced, stored in
a retrieval system or transmitted in any form or by any means electronic,
mechanical, photocopying, recording or otherwise, without prior written
permission of the copyright owner.

The JUMP! logo and the word JUMP! are registered trade marks.

British Library Cataloguing in Publication Data
Watts, Claire
On Safari. - (Jump! starts first look at animals (1))
I. Title II. Series
591.52

PBK ISBN 1-85434-118-9
HBK ISBN 1-85434-132-4

Photo credits:
p. 2-3 Bruce Coleman, p. 5 Bruce Coleman, p. 7 Zefa, p. 9 Zefa, p. 11 NHPA, p. 13 NHPA, p. 15 Zefa,
p. 17 Ardea, p. 19 Zefa, p. 21 Bruce Coleman, back cover NHPA